First US edition 2023
First published by Big Picture Press,
an imprint of Bonnier Books UK, 2022

Library of Congress Catalog Card Number 2022908684
ISBN 978-1-5362-2973-8

22 23 24 25 26 27 TLF 10 9 8 7 6 5 4 3 2 1

Printed in Dongguan, Guangdong, China

For Vincent —BT
For Otis, who loves ducks —CB

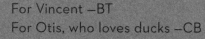

This book was typeset in Core Circus and Neutraface Text.
The illustrations were created digitally.

BIG PICTURE PRESS
an imprint of
Candlewick Press
99 Dover Street
Somerville, Massachusetts 02144

www.candlewick.com

BIRDS
EVERYWHERE

ILLUSTRATED BY BRITTA TECKENTRUP
WRITTEN BY CAMILLA DE LA BEDOYERE

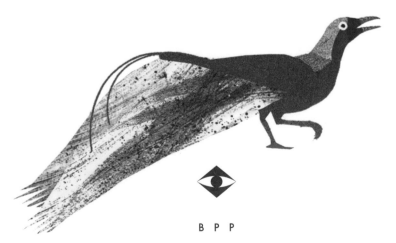

BPP

THERE ARE BIRDS EVERYWHERE

Birds soar through the skies, chatter in treetops, paddle in ponds, and dive into the deep blue sea. Songbirds welcome each new day with a chorus of cheeps and tweets, while dancing birds delight us with their dazzling feathers and fine displays. Birds are also some of the world's greatest travelers and have made their homes from the Arctic in the north to the icy Antarctic in the south—and almost everywhere in between.

Eurasian collared dove

Eurasian golden oriole

Eastern spinebill

King vulture

Kākāpō

Kiwi

African jacana

Greater bird-of-paradise

Blue-footed booby

Weka

Shearwater

Wandering albatross

Arctic tern

Scarlet macaw

Andean condor

European goldfinch

Barn swallow

Harpy eagle

Atlantic puffin

Emperor penguin

Blue jay

Takahē

Black-winged stilt

Eurasian blackbird

All birds have wings and feathers, but not all of them can fly.
Can you guess which birds can't fly?

IT'S A BIRD!
(SO WHAT *IS* THAT?)

There are about 10,000 species of birds around the world, and they all have a beak, two legs, two wings, and a feathered body. Female birds lay eggs with a hard shell, which protects the chick that grows inside. After a few weeks, the eggs hatch and the chicks are looked after until they can take care of themselves.

BONY SKELETONS

Birds are **vertebrates**, which means they have bony skeletons. Muscles are attached to the bones, which also protect a bird's soft organs, such as the heart. The bones in a bird's skeleton are hollow. Extra air sacs sit inside the bones and help birds breathe.

LUNCH BOX

Some birds have a **crop** (a muscular pouch in the throat), where food is stored before it passes into the stomach. The **gizzard** is part of the digestive system, and birds that eat hard food also swallow small stones to help to grind the food into smaller pieces, making it easier to digest.

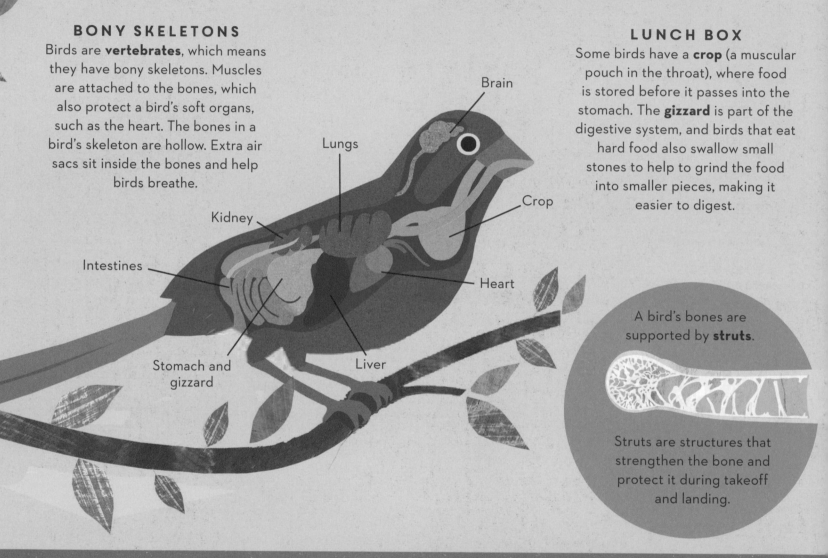

Brain

Lungs

Kidney

Intestines

Stomach and gizzard

Liver

Heart

Crop

A bird's bones are supported by **struts**.

Struts are structures that strengthen the bone and protect it during takeoff and landing.

WHY FLY WHEN IT'S FUN TO RUN?

Before humans brought land mammals, such as cats and dogs, to New Zealand, the birds that lived there had few predators. As bird species evolved within this environment, safely living and nesting on the ground, they gradually lost the ability to fly.

This is the **kākāpō**—one of the world's rarest parrots. It comes out only at night, and it uses its stout legs to walk, jog, or climb.

Kiwis have soft, fluffy feathers. They sniff out worms using nostrils at the tip of their beak. It is so sensitive that it can easily sense a wriggling worm under the soil.

SENSES

Most birds have excellent eyesight and good hearing but do not have strong senses of smell or taste. Their ears are small holes that are hidden below their eyes, protected by feathers.

Wing

Eye

Ear

Beak or bill

Nostril

Feathers (all of a bird's feathers are called its **plumage**)

Breast

Tail

Clawed toes

FLEXIBLE FEET

Bird feet are adapted for walking, perching, and holding. Each foot has two, three, or four toes. Birds' feet are shaped differently depending on the environment where they live.

Ducks spend much of their time in water and have webbed feet that are perfectly suited for swimming.

Songbirds have three toes facing forward and one toe facing back. This arrangement works well for perching on branches.

Jacanas are tropical waders. They can walk on floating lily pads because they have very wide feet that spread their weight.

Female **wekas** stay close to their burrow, where they hide their cup-shaped nest and eggs. Wekas eat almost anything, from seeds and lizards to rotting meat.

Takahēs live in pairs and often mate for life. If one takahē cannot see its partner, it will make a loud cooet call so that the pair can quickly find each other.

BIRDS HAVE BEEN AROUND FOR AGES

Birds have been around for a really long time. Many dinosaurs had colorful feathers, and through the process of evolution, by around 150 million years ago, some feathered species had developed wings. It is believed that they used their wings to fly into trees in order to escape from predators and to find food. Over time, these flying dinosaurs evolved further and became the first birds.

Eoraptor

230 MILLION YEARS AGO

The ancestors of flying birds were dinosaurs that lived on land. Known as **theropods**, these creatures were small, speedy hunters that feasted on other reptiles and bugs.

Anchiornis

Although **Anchiornis** had wings, it probably couldn't fly. Instead, it used its long, feathered limbs to climb trees. This birdlike dinosaur was about 14 inches/35 centimeters long.

Archaeopteryx

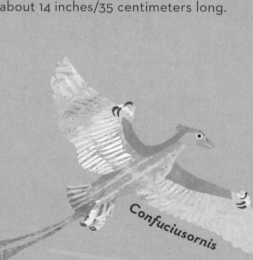

Confuciusornis

Hesperornis

Often called the "first bird," it's thought that **Archaeopteryx** could fly short distances. It had feathers, a long, bony tail, claws on its wings, and a beak that was lined with teeth.

Confuciusornis had reddish-brown feathers and sharp claws. It could glide between trees by spreading its wings, and it may have been able to travel short distances by flapping.

Stubby little wings are no use for flying, but they can be used like paddles to swim. **Hesperornis** was a diving bird that, like a modern **penguin**, swam underwater to catch fish.

Argentavis

Argentavis was a giant bird with a wingspan of 23 feet/ 7 meters. It was a member of a group of predatory birds called "monster birds" and would have dwarfed modern **condors**.

Titanis

Huge "terror birds," such as *Titanis*, couldn't fly, but they used their long legs to chase their prey across the grasslands of what is now known as North America.

Finch

Enormous birds of prey, such as *Teratornis*, were fierce hunters until the last ice age ended around 11,700 years ago. As the global climate changed, habitats and food sources were affected, and *Teratornis*—along with many other large birds—died out.

The first songbirds were perching in trees and singing to their mates more than 50 million years ago. Like modern birds such as *finches*, they probably ate seeds.

Teratornis

Presbyornis

TODAY

There are at least 10,350 species of birds alive today, and scientists now believe that, from the shy *Eurasian golden oriole* to the mighty **eagle owl**, they are all related to dinosaurs.

Presbyornis was a long-legged bird thought to be a prehistoric relative of water-loving birds such as **geese**, **ducks**, and **swans**.

Eurasian golden oriole

WHERE DO BIRDS LIVE?

Birds need a safe place to raise their chicks with plenty of food nearby. They can be found nesting near rivers, coasts, deserts, and grasslands, but are especially abundant in forests and woodlands. In fact, there are more types of birds in forests than in any other habitat.

HIDDEN HOLLOWS

Hornbills, **macaws**, and **owls** often nest inside natural tree holes, but **woodpeckers** use their sharp beak to drill new holes in tree trunks, where they lay their eggs.

KITCHEN PANTRY

Trees provide plenty of food for birds, from seeds, flowers, and fruits to bugs and small reptiles. **Butcher-birds** and **shrikes** first kill their prey, then impale them on twigs or horns for easier eating—they even return later for the leftovers.

BEST FOR NESTS

Tucked away in a leafy tree, a **European goldfinch** nest can be hard to find. That means that eggs and chicks are more likely to survive.

A PLACE TO PERCH

There's a bird's-eye view from a treetop. Perched high up, **Eurasian blackbirds** can look out for food, danger, or a mate.

CAN YOU FIND IT?

Potoos and **frogmouths** have such good camouflage that their brown plumage is hard to spot when they sit perfectly still on a branch. Can you find one of each on this page?

GLOBAL BIRDS

DESERT BIRDS

There's not much water in a desert, but **sandgrouse** have adapted to solve this problem. Males sit in water holes, where their feathers soak up water like a sponge. Then they fly back to the nest, and the chicks suck on their feathers when they are thirsty.

MOUNTAIN BIRDS

Enormous **condors** fly above the Andes Mountains. They use their broad wings to glide on warm air currents, which lift them high into the sky. Some condors have wingspans of more than 10 feet/ 3 meters across.

GRASSLAND BIRDS

Having long legs and swift strides can come in handy in grassland habitats, where lions prowl and there are few places to hide. **Ostriches** are flightless birds, but they can race along the savanna at speeds of 31 miles/50 kilometers per hour.

GROUND BIRDS

Ground birds often have patterned feathers that help them to hide from potential predators. Female **pheasants** have dull brown feathers that camouflage them when they nest. You can easily spot their male partners, as they have much more colorful plumage.

WATER BIRDS

Birds from all over the world gather along the Andalusian coast, in Spain, where the Atlantic Ocean and Mediterranean Sea meet. They find food in the shallow water or wetlands nearby, and they rest before continuing their journeys to places where they will nest and lay eggs.

OCEAN HABITAT

In expanses of open ocean, there aren't many places to stop and rest or to lay eggs. Many seabirds are long-distance travelers that have to fly for hours—or even days—dipping and diving to find food before they reach their coastal homes.

The **skua** is known as a "pirate bird" because it attacks other seabirds and steals food from them.

Large flocks of **shearwaters** skim across the surface of the water looking for fish, shellfish, or squid.

Northern gannets can plunge more than 50 feet/15 meters into the salty ocean to catch fish. Air sacs beneath their chest feathers work like cushions to soften the blow as they hit the water.

COASTAL HABITAT

Coastal birds gather on Andalusia's high cliffs, where they are safe from predators. They hunt fish in the ocean or pick up worms and shellfish that they find in the soft mud when the tide goes out.

Tough shellfish are too hard for most birds to eat, but the **Eurasian oystercatcher** has a strong, blunt beak that can easily crack open hard shells.

WETLAND HABITAT
Wetlands and rivers are home to many birds, but there's enough food for millions of migrating birds passing through, too. These weary travelers enjoy a well-deserved rest before continuing their journeys.

There's a flash of bright yellow as some **Eurasian golden orioles** fly past. These migrating birds nest in trees that grow alongside rivers and wetlands.

Puffins are called "sea parrots" because they stand upright and have colorful faces. They nest on the coast, where they hunt slippery sand eels to feed to their chicks.

CAN YOU FIND IT?
Marsh harriers nest on the ground, hidden by the tall reeds that grow in wetlands. They hunt mice, rats, and voles as well as other birds. Can you find a harrier in its nest?

As it wades through water, the **little egret**'s feet disturb fish, frogs, and bugs, which the bird snaps up with its long beak.

The **black-winged stilt** has longer legs for its size than any other bird. Long legs are useful when wading through shallow water looking for insects, crustaceans, and fish to eat.

THE POWER TO FLY

Flying is a very useful skill for birds. When flying high in the sky, birds have a unique view of the world below—they can travel quickly, find food, or spot new places to nest. Being able to soar up into the sky is also a great way to escape from dangerous predators on the ground.

FANTASTIC FEATHERS

Feathers grow from a bird's skin, similar to the way hair grows from ours. Birds' feathers help them fly, protect their soft skin, and keep them warm. While dull-colored feathers can create a useful camouflage, vibrant colors are good for attracting a mate.

THERE ARE THREE MAIN TYPES OF FEATHERS:

Down feathers are soft and fluffy, providing warmth.

Contour feathers are stiff and cover the bird's body, giving it a smooth shape so the bird glides easily through the air as it flies. This is called **streamlining**.

Flight feathers grow on a bird's wings and tail. They help lift the bird's body into the air.

Down

Contour

Flight

WONDERFUL WINGS

Wings are essential for flight, and their shape and size give scientists clues as to the way a bird flies and its speed.

Wandering albatrosses are not the fastest fliers, but they can stay at sea for years at a time. They have the largest wingspan of any bird—up to a colossal 10 feet/3 meters. Their huge wings allow them to soar on the wind, barely needing to flap.

Birds with pointed wings that curve backward are usually fast fliers. **Swallows** are aerial acrobats that quickly change direction as they dart, dip, and dive to catch flying insects.

Short, rounded wings help small birds, such as **sparrows**, flit easily between trees and shrubs and lift off at speed if a quick escape is needed.

FLOCK IN FLIGHT

There's safety in numbers, so birds often live or travel in groups called **flocks**. It's harder for a predator to attack a large group than it is to attack a single bird.

Starlings gather in large flocks called **murmurations**. As the flock flies, the birds swoop, dive, and change direction together, creating a beautiful bird dance in the sky. Starling flocks often perform their dances in the evening, just before they settle down to sleep for the night.

When one bird starts to change direction, the birds nearest to it follow suit. In the blink of an eye, the message to move spreads across the whole flock, and the group changes shape and flies away in a different direction.

CAN YOU FIND IT?
Flocks of starlings twist and swirl to confuse predators so they can't pick out one starling from the group. Can you find a puzzled **falcon**?

Blue jays make good lookouts. If one member of the flock spies danger, it screeches loudly, telling the others to either escape or mob the potential attacker.

In Africa, **red-billed queleas** gather in flocks of more than one million birds. The largest flocks often form just after the rainy season begins, when there is plenty of food to eat.

FEEDING

Modern birds don't have teeth, but that hasn't stopped them from being able to eat almost every type of food, from crunchy nuts to wriggly worms.

VEGGIE BIRDS

Nuts, seeds, and fruits are nutritious for birds as well as for people.

Any predator that tries to eat a **hooded pitohui** gets a toxic shock! Poisons stored in the bird's skin and feathers come from its diet of poisonous beetles.

The **eastern spinebill** uses its tongue, which has a brushlike tip, to lap up nectar from flowers.

Parrots have very flexible four-toed feet. This **galah**'s toes work like fingers, enabling the bird to grip fruit and lift it to its short, curved beak.

SEAFOOD DIETS

Oceans and rivers are home to tasty bird food such as soft-bodied fish, squid, and worms, as well as crunchier shellfish and crabs.

Most **finches** have short, strong beaks for cracking open nuts and seeds. **Gouldian finches** peck at seeds that fall on the ground.

Pied avocets are waders that swish their long, curved beak from side to side in the water, scooping up worms, shellfish, and insects.

BUG-EATERS

Birds need good eyesight and quick reactions to snap up insects, spiders, and other fast-moving bugs. Having a thin, daggerlike beak also helps with the tricky task of picking up tiny creatures.

Bee-eaters snatch honeybees and other flying insects out of the air. They remove dangerous stingers by rubbing the insects against a twig and then proceed to swallow their prey whole.

UNUSUAL DIETS

Lots of birds eat seeds and fish, but others survive on stranger diets—including meals of blood or rotting meat!

Oxpeckers hitch a ride on the back of large savanna mammals. They eat the parasites that live on the animals, and they also feed on the blood that oozes from the animals' skin where the parasites were feeding.

Long-legged **secretary birds** prey on venomous snakes and are able to kill them from a tall height without getting bitten themselves. They either stomp their prey to death or drop it from a tall height before swooping back down to gobble it up.

The rough pads on an **osprey**'s feet are perfect for gripping slippery fish, which it snatches out of the water. Ospreys carry their food back to their nests or to a perch nearby to eat.

The **redshank** is named after its bright red legs. It uses its long beak to dig worms and shellfish out of soft mud and sand.

BARN OWLS

On a dark summer's night, the eerie screech of a **barn owl** can be heard across fields and around farm buildings. Unlike many owls, which hoot, these pale hunters scream as they fly, which is why they are sometimes known as "ghost owls."

Most birds have eyes on either side of their head, which is useful for seeing all around, but an owl's eyes face forward. This arrangement allows owls to spot small animals at night and work out exactly how far away their prey is.

A barn owl's face is creamy-white, and the feathers around it are shaped like a heart. Scientists think their dish-shaped face helps direct sound toward the owl's ears.

Owls use their talons to grab their prey. They usually return to a perch to eat, swallowing small animals in one gulp.

MEAT-EATERS
Birds that hunt other animals are called **birds of prey**, or **raptors**. Most of these meat-eaters are equipped with sharp eyesight, strong talons, and a hooked beak.

MONKEY-HUNTERS
Deep in the Amazon jungle, monkeys keep an eye out for **harpy eagles**. These huge raptors have powerful legs and talons, enabling them to snatch large creatures like monkeys and sloths straight out of a tree.

A barn owl can pinpoint where any sound is coming from because its ears are set at different levels on each side of its head. These nighttime hunters have such good hearing that they can find small animals in total darkness.

When a barn owl spots some prey, it spreads its wings and tail feathers and hovers silently, waiting for the right moment, then plunges down.

Like many other hunting birds, barn owls attack in silence and take their prey by surprise. Their feathers have soft edges to muffle the sound of their wings flapping.

After a meal, owls regurgitate, or vomit up, pellets made of all the body parts they can't digest, such as feathers, bones, and fur.

CAN YOU FIND IT?
Barn owls mostly hunt small animals such as mice, shrews, and voles. There are five mice hiding in this scene. Can you find them all?

BUSY BUILDERS
Birds of prey often build large, messy nests, and some species return to the same nest year after year, adding more sticks to create enormous piles. The nest of a **bald eagle** can weigh as much as a small elephant! These large birds carry prey back to their huge nests to feed their young.

SCAVENGERS
Vultures feed on the bodies of dead animals that they find. Many of these scavengers have a bald head and neck, which helps them avoid contracting diseases or infections from their rotting meals.

LOVE BIRDS

Male birds are some of the most brilliant and beautiful show-offs in the animal kingdom. They flash their colorful feathers, sing songs, and do dazzling dances to impress females. This behavior is called **courtship**.

When a male **frigate bird** wants to catch a female's eye, he puffs up his red throat. It fills with air and swells like a big red balloon.

Satin bowerbirds seem to love the color blue. Males make a **bower** (an elaborate structure) from sticks and decorate it with any blue objects they find to impress a female. These items can include feathers, paper, beads, and plastic toys.

Male **blue-footed booby** birds wave their bright blue feet, bob their head, and even present females with a gift such as food or a stick. If the females like what they see, they will mate for life.

SHOW-OFFS

Birds of paradise are experts at the art of courtship displays. There are around forty species in total, and most of them live on the tropical island of New Guinea.

The long, glossy, elegant feathers of a male **ribbon-tailed astrapia** show a female that he is healthy and fit. Females prefer to mate with healthy males, as their chicks are more likely to survive.

The male **greater bird-of-paradise** sings to help females find him. His strange songs include calls of *caw-caw-caw*, *wick-wick*, *koo-koo*, and *waak*, and he may even meow like a cat!

When a **Raggiana bird-of-paradise** puts on his courtship display, he dips his head down, spreads out his wings like a colorful fan, and shakes his long, fluffy tail feathers.

The **king bird-of-paradise** has slender tail feathers called **wires**, which normally hang downward. However, during courtship, the male wobbles from side to side on his blue feet and flips the wires up so they wave around behind his head.

It's not just how you dance—it's *where* you dance that matters. The **Wilson's bird-of-paradise** clears the forest floor of any fallen leaves to create a smooth stage where he can perform elaborate dance routines for his potential mate.

This female **Volgelkop superb bird-of-paradise** looks very different from her mate, who turns his feathers into a shiny black cape with a startling blue bib! As he dances, he trots from side to side to keep her attention.

PENGUIN PARADE

Antarctica is the coldest place on earth. It is covered with a thick blanket of ice and snow that stretches out into the Southern Ocean, where it is so cold that even the salt water freezes. Despite the howling winds and blizzards, hardy **emperor penguins** complete a long and dangerous journey each year in order to raise their families.

The long Antarctic winter—which lasts from March to October—is just beginning, and thousands of emperor penguins gather in a huge group called a **colony**. The male penguins find their partners and mate. Each female lays a single egg.

Plants can't grow in this icy wilderness, so the penguins don't make nests. Instead, females transfer the eggs onto the males' feet, where they'll be kept warm and safe.

Together, the colony begins its trek back to the ocean. The penguins will spend the rest of the summer there, eating and fattening up so they are ready to survive the next winter.

By December, the chicks are almost fully grown. Their fluffy gray plumage is gradually being replaced by glossy black and white feathers.

NESTS

Emperor penguins don't build nests, but most birds do. Nests protect eggs from predators and are usually made from plant materials. They come in many shapes and sizes, but a cup shape is the most common.

Swiftlets make tiny nests from dried spit and attach them to cave walls or rafters in empty structures. In some parts of the world, the nests are collected and made into a soup.

In such a desolate landscape, there is no food to be foraged, so the female penguins need to reach the ocean for fish. For some colonies, this can be a grueling 62-mile/ 100-kilometer journey.

In the middle of an Antarctic winter, nights last for more than 24 hours. Males survive for months without food while the females leave the colony to feed on fish. Cold and hungry, the remaining male penguins huddle together for warmth and protection as the worst of the winter weather hits the colony.

In July, female penguins begin to return to the colony with full stomachs. The males and females call out to each other until each bird finds its mate.

It's September and summer is finally on its way. The chicks are growing bigger, and their parents take turns trekking back to the ocean for more food.

Some of the eggs have already begun to hatch. The females feed the chicks with fish that they regurgitate from their stomachs. Their partners can now begin the long journey back to the ocean to eat for the first time in months.

This male **weaverbird** uses grass to weave nests. He hangs upside down beneath a nest and flaps his wings to tempt a female to come and lay her eggs inside.

Ovenbird pairs work together to build a big nest from mud. The female overbird sits on her eggs for fourteen days to keep them warm, in a process called **incubation**.

LONG-DISTANCE TRAVELERS

When the weather turns bad or there's no food to be found, that usually means it's time to make a move. Many birds go on long journeys to find warmer and more protected places to raise their chicks. **Arctic terns** are the world's champion migrators, traveling an astonishing 1.5 million miles/2.4 million kilometers in a lifetime. That's like flying to the moon and back three times!

This epic journey takes an Arctic tern through a year of endless summers, from the far northern Arctic to the far southern Antarctic. The birds can fly more than 56,000 miles/90,000 kilometers in just one year, making this the longest migration of the animal kingdom.

It's the end of summer in the Arctic, the region around the north pole, and it's time for the Arctic terns to fly south. If they don't leave before winter, they will starve or freeze to death.

After flying about 3,700 miles/6,000 kilometers, the birds enjoy a monthlong summer rest on islands in the North Atlantic Ocean.

By May and June, most of the terns have reached the Arctic. It's summer again, and with warm weather and plenty of food, it's a perfect time to lay eggs and care for their chicks.

It's a mystery how migrating birds know how to follow the same route each year. They may recognize places like mountains and coasts, but scientists think they also use the Earth's **magnetic field** as a compass.

For the next five months, the birds focus on eating, growing, and putting on weight as they prepare for the long return journey. The Antarctic winter is fast approaching, and soon it will be time to head north. With strong winds behind them, they can often fly more than 300 miles/500 kilometers a day.

When their well-earned break is over, in September, the Arctic terns continue south. Some birds fly along the coast of Africa while others cross the ocean and fly along South America's coastline.

By November, the Arctic terns have reached the Weddell Sea. It's summer in Antarctica, and they feast on **krill**, the tiny pink shrimplike animals that thrive in these waters.

BIRDS AND PEOPLE

Birds have been a part of culture, mythology, and history for thousands of years, but they also enrich our daily lives with their songs and fascinating behavior. As we become more aware of how important it is to nurture the natural world, we are learning to treasure our feathered friends and take better care of their habitats.

THAT'S EGGSTRA-ORDINARY!

An **ostrich** egg is about 6 inches/ 15 centimeters long and can be made into a giant omelet! **Chickens** and **ostriches** that live on farms lay eggs that are **unfertilized**. This means the eggs don't grow into chicks and can be used as a good source of protein in our diets.

BIRD GODS

The **phoenix** is a mythical bird that the ancient Greeks believed could live for hundreds of years before dying in a blaze of flames and being reborn from the ashes. The ancient Egyptians revered the falcon-headed god, **Horus**. They believed that he protected their rulers, called pharaohs, from evil.

HERO BIRD

A **pigeon** named GI Joe saved the lives of more than one hundred soldiers in World War II. He carried a message to American soldiers that warned them not to bomb a town where the British soldiers had just arrived. GI Joe was awarded a medal for his bravery.

BIRDS IN SCIENCE

People have always wondered what it would be like to fly like a bird. In the fifteenth century, Italian artist and inventor Leonardo da Vinci designed a flying machine called an **ornithopter**. It wasn't until 1903 that the first successful airplane was invented by Wilbur and Orville Wright.

Some drones are designed to look like **herring gulls**. They mimic the way real gulls fly, twisting and flapping their wings to gain height, move forward, and change direction.

BIRD-WATCHING

Bird-watching is one of the world's most popular hobbies. It's fun to learn how to recognize the birds that live around us in gardens and parks and to visit wild places to spot new species.

It's important to observe from a safe distance and to never disturb a bird's nest or touch its eggs and chicks. This is to avoid hurting the animals and spreading diseases between people and birds.

Binoculars, a camera, a notebook, a guidebook, and a pen are useful tools for a bird-watcher.

If you see a bird with a metal ring on one leg, it might be part of a scientific study on migration. Scientists track these birds to learn more about their habitats and migration routes and to discover how well they are coping with climate change, deforestation, and other threats.

Make a note of the bird's size and behavior, looking carefully at its colors and listening to its song. Use this information to identify the bird and find out more about how it lives.

In 1977, a scientist named Irene Pepperberg bought Alex, an **African gray parrot**, from a pet store. She taught him to say more than one hundred words, which he used to "talk" with Dr. Pepperberg. Alex helped scientists discover more about how birds learn new skills and communicate.

When the first bullet trains would speed out of tunnels at 180 miles/300 kilometers per hour, they'd create a loud noise. Engineers copied the long beak of a **kingfisher**—a bird that dives into water without a splash—to solve the noise problem. The new design also made the train more efficient.